SPECIAL
TO GOD

Catherine Butcher

W0007210

Copyright © CWR 2005

Published 2005 by CWR, Waverley Abbey House, Waverley Lane, Farnham, Surrey GU9 8EP, England. Reprinted 2008.
The right of Catherine Butcher to be identified as the author of this work has been asserted by her in accordance with the Copyright, Designs and Patents Act 1988, sections 77 and 78.

All rights reserved. No part of this publication may be reproduced, stored in a retrieval system, or transmitted, in any form or by any means, electronic, mechanical, photocopying, recording or otherwise, without the prior permission in writing of CWR.

See back of book for list of National Distributors.

Unless otherwise indicated, all Scripture references are from the Holy Bible: New International Version (NIV), copyright © 1973, 1978, 1984 by the International Bible Society.

Other versions used are marked:
HCSB: Holman Christian Standard Bible. Copyright © 1999, 2000, 2002, 2003 by Holman Bible Publishers.
The Message: Scripture taken from The Message. Copyright © 1993, 1994, 1995, 1996, 2000, 2001, 2002. Used by permission of NavPress Publishing Group.
NIRV: New International Reader's Version. Copyright © 1996, 1998 by International Bible Society.
ESV: English Standard Version. From The Holy Bible, English Standard Version, published by HarperCollins Publishers © 2001 by Crossway Bibles, a division of Good News Publishers. Used by permission. All rights reserved.
CEV: Contemporary English Version. Copyright © 1995 by American Bible Society.
AV: The Authorised Version

Concept development, editing, design and production by CWR

Printed in China by C&C Offset Printing
ISBN 978-1-85345-508-7

To:

On the occasion of:

Date:

From:

INTRODUCTION

Do you know how special you are?

Maybe a parent or close friend has told you that you're special. Perhaps you have a skill or gift which makes you special. You may have been given this book because of a special occasion in your life. But did you know that you are special to God?

Discover why God thinks you are special as you take inspiration from the Bible verses in this selection. Use some of the prayers to respond to God and allow Him to be involved in your life, bringing comfort, encouragement, direction, peace and power for living. Learn to enjoy a lifelong relationship with God as you get to know His Son, Jesus.

1
SPECIAL TO GOD

Now this is what the LORD says –
the One who created you …
'Do not fear, for I have redeemed you;
 I have called you by your name;
    you are Mine.
I will be with you …
Because you are precious in My sight
and honored, and I love you …'

Isaiah 43:1–2, 4 (HCSB)

Read the promise again:

God created you;
He knows your name;
He is with you
whatever you're facing in life;
you are precious to Him;
He loves you.

You are special

to Him.

Blessed be the God and Father of
our Lord Jesus Christ ... for He chose
us in Him, before the foundation of the
world, to be holy and blameless in His
sight. In love He predestined us to be
adopted through Jesus Christ for Himself,
according to His favour and will ...

Ephesians 1:3–5 (HCSB)

Chosen, longed for,
acceptable,
blameless, loved,
planned ...
Isn't that what we all
want to be?

Use these words from King David's psalm as a prayer to God who loves you and knows you better than you know yourself. You are special to Him.

For it was You who created my inward parts;
You knit me together in my mother's womb.
I will praise You,
because I have been remarkably and
    wonderfully made.
Your works are wonderful,
and I know this very well.
My bones were not hidden from You
when I was made in secret,
when I was formed in the depths of the earth.
Your eyes saw me when I was formless;
all my days were written in Your book
    and planned
before a single one of them began.

Psalm 139:13–16 (HCSB)

This is how much God loved the world:
He gave his Son, his one and only Son.
And this is why: so that no one need be
destroyed; by believing in him, anyone
can have a whole and lasting life.

John 3:16 (*The Message*)

But here is how God
has shown his love for us.
While we were still sinners,
Christ died for us.

Romans 5:8 (NIRV)

When I survey the wondrous cross
On which the Prince of Glory died,
My richest gain I count but loss,
And pour contempt on all my pride.

See from His head, His hands, His feet,
Sorrow and love flow mingled down!
Did e'er such love and sorrow meet,
Or thorns compose so rich a crown?

Were the whole realm of nature mine,
That were an offering far too small;
Love so amazing, so divine,
Demands my soul, my life, my all.

Isaac Watts (1674–1748)

2

LOVED
BY GOD

What marvelous love
the Father has extended
to us! Just look at it –
we're called children
of God! That's who
we really are.

1 John 3:1 (*The Message*)

Human fathers

make mistakes –
but God,
your heavenly Father,
is perfect.
He makes no mistakes.
He has chosen you to be
part of His family.
Being His child
is amazing –
beyond your
wildest dreams.

What is God's love like?

Love is patient, love is kind. It does not
envy, it does not boast, it is not proud.
It is not rude, it is not self-seeking,
it is not easily angered,
it keeps no record of wrongs.
Love does not delight in evil
but rejoices with the truth.
It always protects, always trusts,
always hopes, always perseveres.
Love never fails.

1 Corinthians 13:4–8

How did God show his love for us?
He sent his one and only Son into the
world. He sent him so we could
receive life through him ...
since God loved us that much,
we should also love one another.

1 John 4:9, 11 (NIRV)

Who can separate us

from the love of Christ?
Can affliction or anguish or persecution
or famine or nakedness or danger
or sword?
As it is written ...
No, in all these things we are more
than victorious
through Him who loved us.

For I am persuaded that neither death
    nor life,
nor angels nor rulers,
nor things present, nor things to come,
    nor powers,
nor height, nor depth, nor any other
    created thing
will have the power to separate us
from the love of God that is in Christ
    Jesus our Lord!

Romans 8:35–39 (HCSB)

The steadfast love of the LORD
  never ceases;
his mercies never come to an end;
they are new every morning;
great is your faithfulness.

Lamentations 3:22–23 (ESV)

There are no endings in God's love.
It doesn't diminish with time
... or run out with distance.

Allow that fact to fill your thoughts,
reverberating round your mind
with every step you take today:

'I'm loved ...

I'm loved ...

I'm loved ...'

3

GRACE
OF GOD

The *Compact Oxford English Dictionary* defines grace as the 'free and unearned favour of God'.

You can remember what grace means using its letters to remind you.

Grace is:

God's

Riches

At

Christ's

Expense

... we see Jesus,
who was made a little lower
than the angels,
now crowned with
glory and honour
because he suffered death,
so that by the grace of God
he might taste death
for everyone.

Hebrews 2:9

God's grace

through Jesus offers us:
forgiveness for everything
we have ever done wrong,
acceptance, love and power
to live God's way
from now on.

Amazing grace! How sweet the sound
That saved a wretch like me!
I once was lost, but now am found;
Was blind, but now I see.

The Lord has promised good to me,
His Word my hope secures;
He will my Shield and Portion be,
As long as life endures.

John Newton, *Olney Hymns* (London: W. Oliver, 1779).

The LORD is compassionate
and gracious,
slow to anger and full of faithful love.
He will not always accuse us
or be angry forever.
He has not dealt with us as our sins
deserve
or repaid us according to our offences.

For as high as the heavens are above
    the earth,
so great is His faithful love
toward those who fear Him.
As far as the east is from the west,
so far has He removed
our transgressions from us.

Psalm 103:8–12 (HCSB)

We don't deserve
anything from God –
but our loving heavenly
Father wants us to enjoy
being with Him. His
grace towards us makes
it possible for us to enjoy
His company – forever.

But God is faithful and fair.
If we admit that we have sinned,
he will forgive us our sins.
He will forgive every
wrong thing we have done.
He will make us pure.

1 John 1:9 (NIRV)

4

COMFORTED BY GOD

God says:

'As a mother

comforts her child,

so will I

comfort you ...'

Isaiah 66:13

God, your heavenly
Father, wants to be
your comforter.
Whatever life
throws at you,
He will be with you.

When Jesus began
His public ministry,
He read from these verses in Isaiah.
They apply to you too if you are
broken-hearted, mourning
or in despair.

The Spirit of the Lord GOD is on Me,
because the LORD has anointed Me
to bring good news to the poor.
He has sent Me to heal the broken-hearted,
to proclaim liberty to the captives,
and freedom to the prisoners;
to proclaim the year of the LORD's favor,
and the day of our God's vengeance;
to comfort all who mourn,
to provide for those who mourn in Zion;
to give them a crown of beauty instead of ashes,
festive oil instead of mourning,
and splendid clothes instead of despair.
And they will be called righteous trees,
planted by the LORD,
to glorify Him.

Isaiah 61:1–3 (HCSB)

Give praise to the God and Father of our Lord Jesus Christ! He is the Father who gives tender love. All comfort comes from him. He comforts us in all our troubles. Now we can comfort others when they are in trouble. We ourselves have received comfort from God. We share the sufferings of Christ. We also share his comfort.

2 Corinthians 1:3–5 (NIRV)

Rest-and-be-thankful
is the name given to viewpoints
in some of Britain's most scenic
beauty spots; it's also
a recipe for God's comfort:
receive God's rest and be thankful
for all He has done for you.
Ask God to help you to see your life –
with all its ups and downs –
from His eternal perspective.

He will wipe every tear from their eyes. There will be no more death or mourning or crying or pain, for the old order of things has passed away.

Revelation 21:4

Turn your longing for comfort into a prayer like this psalm written by King David:

O God, you are my God, earnestly
    I seek you;
my soul thirsts for you, my body
    longs for you,
in a dry and weary land where there
    is no water ...
Because your love is better than life,
    my lips will glorify you.

Psalm 63:1, 3

5

ENCOURAGEMENT

As Christians
we are never alone.
Jesus makes it possible
for us to draw near to
God. He promises to give
us His Holy Spirit,
to be with us forever.

Come near to God

and he will come

near to you.

James 4:8

... Christ with me,
Christ before me,
Christ behind me,
Christ in me,
Christ beneath me,
Christ above me ...

Patrick, Apostle of Ireland (387–493).

Do not fear, for I am with you;
do not be afraid, for I am your God.
I will strengthen you; I will help you;
I will hold on to you with My righteous
    right hand.

Isaiah 41:10 (HCSB)

How many people really know you?
It's rare for us to have more than two or
three others who get to know us deeply.
But God knows you – and He still loves
you. Read what King David wrote about
how intimately we are known by God ...
let your spirit thrive on this
encouragement:

LORD, You have searched me
   and known me.
You know when I sit down and when
   I stand up;
You understand my thoughts from far away.
You observe my travels and my rest;
You are aware of all my ways.
Before a word is on my tongue,
You know all about it, LORD.
You have encircled me;
You have placed Your hand on me.
This extraordinary knowledge is beyond me.

Psalm 139:1–6 (HCSB)

May our Lord Jesus Christ
himself and God our Father, who loved
us and by his grace gave us eternal
encouragement and good hope, encourage
your hearts and strengthen you in every
good deed and word.

2 Thessalonians 2:16–17

According to the
Concise Oxford Dictionary,
to encourage is to
'give courage to'; 'urge';
'reward'; 'promote'; 'assist'.

What do you need God's
encouragement for today?
God's encouragement
is always available for you.

6

DIRECTION
FROM GOD

Trust in the LORD with all
　　your heart,
and do not rely on your own
　　understanding;
think about Him in all your ways,
and He will guide you on the right paths.

Proverbs 3:5–6 (HCSB)

Don't know what to do?
Ask God to guide you,
then take steps forward.
Don't be surprised if God opens
up unexpected opportunities
or brings you to
an occasional dead end.
If you invite Him to guide you,
He is committed to making sure
you move in the right direction.

Dearest Lord,

may I see You today ...
Though You hide Yourself behind
the unattractive disguise
of the irritable, the exacting,
the unreasonable,
may I still recognise You, and say,
'Jesus, my patient,
how sweet it is to serve you.'

Mother Teresa of Calcutta (1910–1997)

The LORD will keep you from
    all harm –
he will watch over your life;
the LORD will watch over your coming and
    going both now and for evermore.

Psalm 121:7–8

If any of you
lacks wisdom,
he should ask God,
who gives generously
to all without finding fault,
and it will be given to him.

James 1:5

Guide me, O Thou great Redeemer ...
Pilgrim through this barren land.
I am weak, but Thou art mighty;
Hold me with Thy powerful hand.
Bread of heaven, bread of heaven,
Feed me till I want no more;
Feed me till I want no more.

William Williams, *Hallelujah* (Bristol, England: 1745)

In his Christmas Day broadcast of 1939, with the country at war, King George VI challenged the nation to trust God with these words:
'I said to the man who stood at the Gate of the Year, "Give me a light that I may tread safely into the unknown." And he replied, "Go out into the darkness, and put your hand into the Hand of God. That shall be to you better than light, and safer than a known way."'

We trust the same God. Put your hand into His and He will lead you.

Your word

is a lamp to my

feet and a light

for my path.

Psalm 119:105

7

PEACE
FROM GOD

May the God of hope fill
you with all joy and peace
as you trust in him, so
that you may overflow
with hope by the power
of the Holy Spirit.

Romans 15:13

Filling and overflowing

are the words used to describe
God's peace:
filling means there's no room
for anything else –
no fear, stress, anxiety;
overflowing means other people
will be affected by the peace God
pours into your life.
God gives this peace as a gift.
Unwrap it today.

The LORD is my shepherd;
there is nothing I lack.
He lets me lie down in green pastures;
He leads me beside quiet waters.
He renews my life;
He leads me along the right paths
for His name's sake.
Even when I go through the darkest valley,
I fear no danger,
for You are with me;
Your rod and Your staff – they comfort me.

You prepare a table before me
in the presence of my enemies;
You anoint my head with oil;
my cup overflows.
Only goodness and faithful love will
    pursue me
all the days of my life,
and I will dwell in the house of the LORD
as long as I live.

Psalm 23 (HCSB)

Let the peace
that Christ gives
rule in your
hearts.

Colossians 3:15 (NIRV)

Notice that little word

'let'… *Let* Christ's peace rule.
Don't let work, busy lives,
pressing engagements rule your life.
Let go of your own agenda.
Let God have priority.
Let God lead you.
His agenda includes rest
and brings peace,
even in difficult or busy times.

Don't worry

about anything,
but pray about everything.
With thankful hearts offer up
your prayers and requests to God.
Then, because you belong
to Christ Jesus, God will bless you
with peace that no one can
completely understand.
And this peace will control
the way you think and feel.

Philippians 4:6–7 (CEV)

We serve a supernatural God. As human beings we can allow circumstances to control the way we think and feel. But God is not limited by circumstances. Give your situation to God. Ask Him to tackle the issues you face ... and be thankful that

the God who created

the universe has your

best interests close to

His heart.

8
POWER
FROM GOD

I can do everything

through him

who gives me strength.

Philippians 4:13

And if the Spirit of him
who raised Jesus from the dead
is living in you,
he who raised Christ from the dead
will also give life to your mortal bodies
through his Spirit, who lives in you.

Romans 8:11

*What an amazing thought that God's Spirit
is available to us always to give us the power
to live our daily lives to the full.*

The God who
created us
is all-powerful.
Ask Him
for the strength
you need.

For I know that my redeemer liveth, and that he shall stand at the latter day upon the earth ... though ... worms destroy this body, yet in my flesh shall I see God ...

Job 19:25–26 (AV)

God's whole nature is living in Christ in human form. Because you **belong to Christ**, you have everything you need. He is the ruler over every power and authority.

Colossians 2:9–10 (NIRV)

May you be

strengthened

with all power,

according to

His glorious might ...

Colossians 1:11 (HCSB)

Power cannot be grasped.

Jesus gave up His right to power, but now
holds all power in heaven and on earth.

In his very nature he was God.
But he did not think that being equal with God
    was something he should hold on to.
Instead, he made himself nothing.
He took on the very nature of a servant.
He was made in human form …
He obeyed God completely, even though it led
    to his death.
In fact, he died on a cross.

So God lifted him up to the highest place.
He gave him the name that is above
    every name.
When the name of Jesus is spoken, everyone's
    knee will bow to worship him.
Every knee in heaven and on earth and under
    the earth will bow to worship him.
Everyone's mouth will say that Jesus Christ
    is Lord.
And God the Father will receive the glory.

Philippians 2:6–11 (NIRV)

9

ENJOYING GOD

My soul, praise the LORD,
and all that is within me, praise His
   holy name.
My soul, praise the LORD,
and do not forget all His benefits.

He forgives all your sin;
He heals all your diseases.
He redeems your life from the Pit;
He crowns you with faithful love
   and compassion.
He satisfies you with goodness;
your youth is renewed like the eagle.

Psalm 103:1–5 (HCSB)

'... *all* that is within me,

praise ...'.

Do you normally use your voice
to praise God?
Put your mind to work.
How else can you praise God?

Command those
who are rich in this present world
not to be arrogant
nor to put their hope in wealth,
which is so uncertain,
but to put their hope in God,
who richly provides us
with everything for our enjoyment.

1 Timothy 6:17

In the rich Western world, advertisers
love to paint an idealised picture of life:
wealthy, healthy people enjoying life,
without a care in the world. God is the
stern observer; all don'ts and no fun.
Reality couldn't be more different.
God loves to lavish us with everything
we need for lasting enjoyment.
He says 'Yes' to peaceful, healthy living.
He designed us to live that way,
within the safety of His boundaries.

What do you enjoy?

How very rich are God's wisdom
and knowledge!
How he judges is more than we can
understand!
The way he deals with people is more than
we can know …
All things come from him.
All things are directed by him.
All things are for his good.
May God be given the glory forever!

Romans 11:33, 35–36 (NIRV)

The chief end of man
is to glorify God
and to enjoy Him
forever.

Westminster Shorter Catechism, 1648

God, of Your goodness
give me Yourself,
for You are enough
for me.
And only in You
do I have everything.

Julian of Norwich (1342–1416)

Trust in the LORD and do good;
dwell in the land and enjoy safe pasture.
Delight yourself in the LORD
and he will give you the desires
of your heart.

Psalm 37:3–4

10
SAVED
BY GOD

David, the psalm-writer, made mistakes as we all do. But, rather than wallowing in a pit of depression, he turned to God and asked for help. He knew he deserved nothing from God, but found God lifted him up. God's grace means He will do the same for you, if you ask.

I waited patiently for the L<small>ORD</small>,
and He turned to me and heard my cry
    for help.
He brought me up from a desolate pit,
out of the muddy clay,
and set my feet on a rock,
making my steps secure.
He put a new song in my mouth,
a hymn of praise to our God.

Psalm 40:1–3 (HCSB)

At one time

we too acted like fools.

We didn't obey God …

We were controlled by

all kinds of longings and

pleasures …

... But the kindness and love of God our Saviour appeared ... He saved us by washing away our sins. We were born again. The Holy Spirit gave us new life. God poured out the Spirit on us freely because of what Jesus Christ our Saviour has done.
His grace made us right with God.
So now we have received the hope of eternal life as God's children.

Titus 3:3–7 (NIRV)

Praise be to the God and Father of our Lord Jesus Christ! In his great mercy he has given us new birth into a living hope through the resurrection of Jesus Christ from the dead, and into an inheritance that can never perish, spoil or fade – kept in heaven for you ...

1 Peter 1:3–4

Are you saving for

the future?

God invites you to invest

in an eternal future

with Him.

When I was in trouble, I called out
  to the Lord.
I cried to my God for help.
From his temple he heard my voice.
My cry for help reached his ears ...
He reached down from heaven. He took
  hold of me.
He lifted me out of deep waters.
He saved me from my powerful enemies.
He set me free from those who were too
  strong for me.

They stood up to me when I was in trouble.
But the Lord helped me.
He brought me out into a wide and safe
    place.
He saved me because he was pleased
    with me.

Psalm 18:6, 16–19 (NIRV)

Your response

✝

Do you really know that you are
special to God?
Are you aware of His love for you ... love shown
by Jesus' life, death and resurrection?
Have you unwrapped the gift of God's grace?

God wants to give you so much ...
His comfort, encouragement, direction,
peace and power for living.
You can enjoy life now and eternally with Him.

The God who made our world
and everything in it,
also made you and knows you
in amazing detail.

You can't hide anything from Him.

He knows where you live …

how you live …

He even knows your future.

Don't be tempted to run or hide from Him.

Respond to His love.

Enjoy His embrace.

Party in His presence.

Don't wait to start your relationship with God.

Talk to Him – that's what prayer is:

talking to God.

You don't need to use special words.

Ask God to turn your life around,

so you can live your life His way.

Tell Him you are sorry for living life
your own way, without Him.
Thank God for His Son Jesus, who died to
make it possible for you to know Him.
Ask Him to give you a new life – the life He
gives when His Holy Spirit comes
to live in you.
Find a church where you can be part
of God's family, loving God and putting
His book, the Bible, into practice.

NATIONAL DISTRIBUTORS

UK: (and countries not listed below)
CWR, Waverley Abbey House, Waverley Lane, Farnham, Surrey
GU9 8EP. Tel: (01252) 784700 Outside UK (44) 1252 784700

AUSTRALIA: CMC Australasia, PO Box 519, Belmont,
Victoria 3216. Tel: (03) 5241 3288 Fax: (03) 5241 3290

CANADA: David C Cook Distribution Canada, PO Box 98, 55
Woodslee Avenue, Paris, Ontario N3L 3E5. Tel: 1800 263 2664

GHANA: Challenge Enterprises of Ghana, PO Box 5723, Accra.
Tel: (021) 222437/223249 Fax: (021) 226227

HONG KONG: Cross Communications Ltd, 1/F, 562A Nathan
Road, Kowloon. Tel: 2780 1188 Fax: 2770 6229

INDIA: Crystal Communications, 10-3-18/4/1, East Marredpalli,
Secunderabad – 500026, Andhra Pradesh.
Tel/Fax: (040) 27737145

KENYA: Keswick Books and Gifts Ltd, PO Box 10242, Nairobi.
Tel: (02) 331692/226047 Fax: (02) 728557

MALAYSIA: Salvation Book Centre (M) Sdn Bhd, 23 Jalan SS
2/64, 47300 Petaling Jaya, Selangor.
Tel: (03) 78766411/78766797 Fax: (03) 78757066/78756360

NEW ZEALAND: CMC Australasia, PO Box 303298, North
Harbour, Auckland 0751. Tel: 0800 449 408 Fax: 0800 449 049

NIGERIA: FBFM, Helen Baugh House, 96 St Finbarr's College
Road, Akoka, Lagos.
Tel: (01) 7747429/4700218/825775/827264

PHILIPPINES: OMF Literature Inc, 776 Boni Avenue, Mandaluyong City. Tel: (02) 531 2183 Fax: (02) 531 1960

SINGAPORE: Alby Commercial Enterprises Pte Ltd, 95 Kallang Avenue #04-00, AIS Industrial Building, 339420. Tel: (65) 629 27238 Fax: (65) 629 27235

SOUTH AFRICA: Struik Christian Books, 80 MacKenzie Street, PO Box 1144, Cape Town 8000. Tel: (021) 462 4360 Fax: (021) 461 3612

SRI LANKA: Christombu Publications (Pvt) Ltd, Bartleet House, 65 Braybrooke Place, Colombo 2. Tel: (9411) 2421073/2447665

TANZANIA: CLC Christian Book Centre, PO Box 1384, Mkwepu Street, Dar es Salaam. Tel/Fax: (022) 2119439

USA: David C Cook Distribution Canada, PO Box 98, 55 Woodslee Avenue, Paris, Ontario N3L 3E5, Canada. Tel: 1800 263 2664

ZIMBABWE: Word of Life Books (Pvt) Ltd, Christian Media Centre, 8 Aberdeen Road, Avondale, PO Box A480 Avondale, Harare. Tel: (04) 333355 or 091301188

For email addresses, visit the CWR website: www.cwr.org.uk
CWR is a Registered Charity – Number 294387
CWR is a Limited Company registered in England – Registration Number 1990308

Day and Residential Courses
Counselling Training
Leadership Development
Biblical Study Courses
Regional Seminars
Ministry to Women
Daily Devotionals
Books and Videos
Conference Centre

Trusted all Over the World

CWR HAS GAINED A WORLDWIDE reputation as a centre of excellence for Bible-based training and resources. From our headquarters at Waverley Abbey House, Farnham, England, we have been serving God's people for over 40 years with a vision to help apply God's Word to everyday life and relationships. The daily devotional *Every Day with Jesus* is read by nearly a million readers an issue in more than 150 countries, and our unique courses in biblical studies and pastoral care are respected all over the world. Waverley Abbey House provides a conference centre in tranquil setting.

For free brochures on our seminars and courses, conference facilities, or a catalogue of CWR resources, please contact us at the following address:

CWR, Waverley Abbey House, Waverley Lane, Farnham, Surrey GU9 8EP, UK

Telephone: +44 (0)1252 784700
Email: mail@cwr.org.uk
Website: www.cwr.org.uk

CWR Applying God's Word
to everyday life and relationships